Learning about Cats

THE
MANX CAT

by Joanne Mattern

Consultant:
Sherman Ross
President
American Manx Club

CAPSTONE
HIGH-INTEREST
BOOKS

an imprint of Capstone Press
Mankato, Minnesota

Library of Congress Cataloging-in-Publication Data
Mattern, Joanne, 1963–
    The Manx cat/by Joanne Mattern.
    p. cm.—(Learning about cats)
    Includes bibliographical references (p. 45) and index.
    Summary: Discusses the history, development, habits, and care of Manx cats.
    ISBN 0-7368-1301-2 (hardcover)
    1. Manx cat—Juvenile literature. [1. Manx cat. 2. Cats.] I. Title. II. Series.
SF449.M36 M38 2003
636.8'22—dc21   2001008338

Editorial Credits
Gillia Olson, editor; Karen Risch, product planning editor; Linda Clavel,
    series designer and illustrator; Gene Bentdahl, book designer; Jo Miller,
    photo researcher

Photo Credits
Chanan Photography, cover, 4, 14, 16, 19, 22, 27, 28, 35, 37
Leslie Falteisek/Clacritter Designs, 38
Norvia Behling, 8, 20, 30, 32
Photo by Mark McCullough, 40–41
Sandie Morris, 6, 10
Sherman Ross, 13
www.ronkimballstock.com, 24

1 2 3 4 5 6 07 06 05 04 03 02

Table of Contents

Quick Facts about the Manx 4

Chapter 1   The Manx Cat 7

Chapter 2   Development of the Breed . . . 11

Chapter 3   Today's Manx 17

Chapter 4   Owning a Manx 21

Chapter 5   Caring for a Manx 29

Photo Diagram 40

Quick Facts about Cats 42

Words to Know 44

To Learn More 45

Useful Addresses 46

Internet Sites 47

Index 48

Quick Facts about the Manx

Description

Size: Manx cats are medium-sized, muscular cats.

Weight: Most adult Manx cats weigh between 7 and 13 pounds (3.2 and 5.9 kilograms).

Physical features: A Manx cat has a wide head with round cheeks. Its back is rounded. A Manx may have a long tail, a stubby tail, a riser tail,

or no tail. A Manx has a double coat.
It can be shorthaired or longhaired.
Some cat associations consider
longhaired Manx cats a separate
breed called Cymric.

Color: Manx cats can be many colors and
patterns. Black, red, brown, bi-color, and
striped tabbies are common.

Development
**Place of
origin:**   The Manx breed comes from the Isle of
Man. This island is located in the Irish
Sea between Great Britain and Ireland.

**History of
breed:**   The Manx breed began about 300 years
ago from a genetic mutation. The Manx
was one of the earliest registered breeds
in Europe. People brought the Manx to
North America in 1899.

Numbers: In 2001, the Cat Fanciers' Association
(CFA) registered 329 Manx cats. Owners
who register their Manx list the cats'
breeding records with an official club.
The CFA is North America's largest
organization of cat breeders.

Chapter 1

The Manx Cat

The Manx is one of the oldest cat breeds. The Manx has long been known for its friendliness.

Appearance

Manx cats can have a long tail, a stumpy tail, a riser tail, or no tail. Manx cats with full tails are called longies. Some Manx have a short, stumpy tail. These cats are called stumpies. Manx cats with no tail have a hollow at the end of their backbone. These Manx are called rumpies.

Another type of Manx has a small bump where a tail normally starts. The bump is made of a strong, rubbery tissue called cartilage. These Manx are called risers.

Only rumpies and risers can compete at cat shows. Stumpies and longies cannot be shown.

These Manx cats live on the Isle of Man. Manx cats can have one of four tail lengths.

Manx cats are good jumpers.

People do breed stumpies and longies. They
also make good pets.

A Manx cat looks round. The cat's back legs
are longer than its front legs. The cat's back
curves up toward its back legs. A Manx also
has a round head and round cheeks.

The Manx is a medium-sized cat. Females
weigh between 7 and 11 pounds (3.2 and
5 kilograms). Most males weigh between
10 and 13 pounds (4.5 and 5.9 kilograms).

8

Manx cats have a double coat of fur. Their undercoat is dense and soft. Their outer coat is glossy and smooth. Longhaired Manx have a long, silky outer coat.

The Cat Fanciers' Association (CFA) considers shorthaired and longhaired Manx as the same breed. But other cat associations consider longhaired Manx a separate breed. The International Cat Association (TICA) and the Canadian Cat Association (CCA) classify longhaired Manx as Cymric.

Personality

Manx cats are smart and playful. Some Manx cats have learned to open doors. Their powerful hindquarters make them good jumpers and fast runners. Manx cats get along well with children. They also enjoy being around other cats and dogs.

Manx cats can become very close to their owners. Some Manx cats do not adjust well to a new owner. But some Manx do adjust well to others.

Chapter 2

Development of the Breed

The Manx cat developed on the Isle of Man. This island lies between Great Britain and Ireland. The Manx is the only cat bred for taillessness. People have made up several myths about the Manx. These stories try to explain why some Manx have no tail.

Manx Myths

One Manx myth involves the story of Noah's ark in the Christian Bible. Noah was saving two of every animal from a great flood. The Manx cat was late getting onto the ark. Noah was in a hurry to sail away. As the Manx came through the door, Noah accidentally slammed the ark's door on the cat's tail. The tail was cut off. All Manx from then on had no tails.

These Manx cats from the Isle of Man probably are descendants of the original Manx cats.

Another myth says that Viking warriors invaded the Isle of Man in the A.D. 800s. These warriors decorated their helmets with animal tails. Female Manx cats bit off their kittens' tails to keep the kittens safe. To this day, some cats on the Isle of Man have no tails.

In 1588, ships from Spain attacked England. Some people think that tailless cats swam to the Isle of Man from one of these Spanish ships. But there are no records of tailless cats in Spain.

Yet another Manx myth says that the Manx is a cross between a cat and a rabbit. When they run, some Manx cats hop like rabbits do. But a cat and a rabbit cannot mate and produce offspring.

Heredity and Genetics

Manx myths can be entertaining. But they are not true. A genetic mutation caused taillessness in Manx cats. A genetic mutation causes part of an animal's body to develop in a different way than normal. This mutation can be passed down to the animal's offspring.

This Manx, Shamen, had good genetics. He produced 16 offspring that won CFA Grand Championships.

Animals that lived on the Isle of Man had little contact with animals from other parts of the world. Animals could not travel easily to the island. The mutation that caused tailless cats was able to spread throughout the island's cat population. More and more cats inherited the mutation and were born without tails.

Gaining Popularity

Records of Manx cats on the Isle of Man begin about 300 years ago. In 1810, British painter Joseph Turner wrote that he had seven Manx cats that came from the Isle of Man.

People first exhibited Manx cats in European cat shows in the 1870s. These cats competed in the domestic class with breeds such as the British Shorthair. These early Manx cats looked much like today's Manx. Some of them had an uneven, hopping walk because their back legs were longer than their front legs. Today, breeders try to breed cats that walk normally.

A Manx cat first competed at a U.S. cat show in 1899. In 1958, a Manx cat became CFA Grand Champion for the first time. This cat was Mrs. Kelly of An-Si from Pittsburgh, Pennsylvania. Over the years, Manx cats have won other important championships and awards. Today, this breed is a popular show cat.

Manx cats continue to compete in and win cat shows.

Chapter 3

Today's Manx

Today's Manx looks very much like the Manx of 300 years ago. These round, powerful cats can make excellent show cats and pets.

Breed Standards

Judges look for specific physical features when they judge a Manx at a cat show. These features are called the breed standard.

A Manx's body is round and solid. Its body has sturdy bones and powerful muscles. Its back curves up from shoulders to rump. Its back legs are longer than its front legs. Show cats must have either no tail or only a small bump of cartilage at the end of the spine.

Manx cats that compete in cat shows must have either no tail or only a riser.

The Manx's head is large, with round cheeks. Its eyes are large and round. Its ears are wide at the base and round at the tips.

A Manx cat has a double coat. The undercoat is short and dense. A shorthaired Manx's outer fur is glossy and hard to the touch. Longhaired Manx have silky hair.

Colors

Manx cats' fur comes in almost every cat color and pattern. Common colors are white, black, cream, silver, blue, and red. Blue is a shade of gray. Red is a shade of orange.

The striped tabby coat, tortoiseshell coat, and tri-colored calico coat also are common. Tortoiseshell cats' fur appears to be a mixture of black and red. Calico cats' coats have patches of three colors. The most common colors are black, red, and white.

The CFA does not allow cats with pointed colors to be shown. Pointed means that the cat has a light coat with darker areas around the ears, face, paws, and tail. TICA accepts pointed Manx cats in shows.

This calico longhaired Manx has patches of black, red, and white.

Chapter 4

Owning a Manx

People can adopt a Manx cat from several places. They can purchase Manx from breeders or pet stores. They can sometimes adopt Manx from animal shelters or rescue organizations.

Manx Breeders
People who want a purebred Manx should go to a breeder. Most breeders register their cats and kittens. Registered cats have papers that list their parents' names and the breeder's name. Cats need these papers to compete at cat shows.

Often, the breeder can show potential owners the parents of a kitten. The buyer can get an idea of how the kitten will look and behave when it is grown.

People who want a purebred Manx kitten should go to a breeder.

Breeders often own a kitten's parents. Owners may see how a kitten will look or behave when it is grown.

Many Manx breeders live in the United States and Canada. These breeders often can be found at cat shows. They usually are happy to talk to people about their cats.

Cat magazines also are good places to find breeders' advertisements. These ads include names, addresses, and phone numbers of breeders. Another source for Manx breeders is the Internet.

People should be sure to check the breeder's references. Other people who have bought cats from a breeder can tell of their experiences. People also should get the cat's medical history before they buy a Manx.

Pet Stores

A pet store is another place to find Manx cats. Store workers may refer people to Manx breeders if the store has no Manx cats.

Pet stores that provide good care to animals will meet certain standards. Good pet stores get animals from a respectable breeder. The animals look healthy and alert. The pet store has the animals' medical records. The animal's cages are large, clean, and comfortable. Good pet stores provide the animals with plenty of food, toys, and fresh water.

Animal Shelters

Shelters can be an inexpensive place to buy a Manx. Animal shelters keep unwanted animals and try to find homes for them. Many more

Rescue organizations often have pet-quality cats for adoption, like this stumpy Manx.

animals are brought to shelters than there are people available to adopt them.

Animals that are not adopted often are euthanized. Shelter workers euthanize animals by injecting them with substances that stop their breathing or heartbeat. Many people adopt pets from shelters so they can save the pets' lives.

Most shelters charge only a small fee to adopt an animal. Local veterinarians often provide discounts on medical services for shelter animals.

Animal shelters usually do not have purebred cats such as the Manx. Shelters often have mixed-breed pets available for adoption. Shelter workers may know little about the animals' parents, health, or behavior. Some cats may have unknown medical or behavioral problems.

Despite these problems, animal shelters have many good pets available. Many owners do not plan to breed or show their cats. Shelter cats can be a good choice for these people.

Rescue Organizations

People interested in adopting a Manx may want to contact a rescue organization. Rescue organizations try to find homes for unwanted and neglected pets.

Rescue organizations are similar to animal shelters. But rescue organizations usually specialize in certain pet breeds. They rarely euthanize the animals. Instead, these places keep pets until people adopt them.

Pets from rescue organizations usually are less expensive than pets from breeders. Rescue organizations may offer registered Manx cats. Workers at rescue organizations often have information about the animals' backgrounds.

People can find information about rescue organizations in several ways. These organizations often have Internet sites. They also may advertise in magazines or newspapers. Animal shelters also may refer people to rescue organizations.

Manx rescue organizations may offer purebred, registered Manx cats.

Chapter 5

Caring for a Manx

Responsible owners can help their Manx cats live long, healthy lives. Manx can live 15 years or more with proper care.

Feeding

Like all cats, Manx cats need high-quality food to stay healthy and strong. Supermarkets and pet stores sell cat food that provides a healthy diet. Owners may feed their Manx dry or moist food.

Dry food usually is less expensive than moist food. It does not spoil if it is left out for long periods of time. The rough texture of dry food helps clean cats' teeth.

Some owners feed their cats moist cat food. Moist food should not be left out for more than

This Manx kitten can live 15 years or more with proper care.

Owners can feed their Manx dry or moist cat food.

one hour. It can spoil easily. Owners who feed their cats moist food usually feed their adult cats twice each day.

Different cats may prefer different types of food. Veterinarians can tell owners which type of food is best for their cats.

Like all cats, Manx need to drink plenty of water to stay healthy. Owners should make sure their Manx's bowl is always filled with fresh, clean water.

Indoor and Outdoor Cats

Some cat owners allow their cats to roam outdoors. This practice is not safe. Outdoor cats can catch serious diseases from other cats. Cars and other animals can injure outdoor cats.

Owners who keep their cat inside must give it a litter box. Litter boxes are filled with small bits of clay called litter. Cats use litter boxes to eliminate waste.

Cats are clean animals. They often refuse to use a dirty litter box. Owners should remove waste from the box each day and change the litter often to keep the box clean.

Both indoor and outdoor cats scratch objects. Cats mark their territories by leaving their scent on objects they scratch. Cats also scratch to release tension and keep their claws sharp. Owners should provide their Manx with a scratching post. The Manx then may not scratch carpet, furniture, or curtains. Owners can buy a scratching post at a pet store or make one from wood and carpet.

Nail Care

The tip of a cat's claw is called the nail. Like other cats, a Manx should have its nails

Owners should begin to trim a Manx's nails when it is a kitten.

trimmed every few weeks with a special nail clipper. Cats with trimmed nails cause less damage to carpet and furniture. Cats with trimmed nails rarely develop ingrown nails. Ingrown nails can occur when a cat's claws grow into the bottom of the paw. This growth can cause serious and painful infections.

An owner should begin to trim a Manx's nails when it is a kitten. The kitten will become used to having its nails trimmed as it grows older.

Dental Care

All cats need regular dental care to protect their teeth and gums from plaque. This coating of bacteria and saliva causes tooth decay and gum disease. Owners should brush their Manx's teeth at least once each week. Owners should use a special toothbrush made for cats or a soft cloth. Owners should brush their Manx's teeth with toothpaste made for cats. Owners should never use toothpaste made for people on a cat. It can make cats sick.

As a Manx grows older, regular brushing may not be enough to remove the plaque from its teeth. A veterinarian should clean an older Manx's teeth each year.

Grooming

Shorthaired Manx cats need little grooming. They should be brushed once each week. Owners should use a soft bristle brush to remove loose hair. After brushing, owners should use a comb to smooth out the cat's fur.

Longhaired Manx may require daily brushing. Cats' fur can sometimes form a tangled mass called a mat. Mats are more common in longhaired Manx. Cat owners should be very careful if they remove a mat from a cat's fur. They could damage their Manx's fur and skin. Owners can ask a veterinarian or a groomer to take out the mats. Groomers are trained to bathe, trim, brush, and comb pets' coats.

Good grooming helps prevent hairballs. A cat swallows loose pieces of fur when it washes itself. This fur can form a ball in the cat's stomach. The cat then vomits the hairball. Large hairballs can block a cat's digestive system. These hairballs require surgery to be removed. Brushing removes loose fur before a cat can swallow it. Owners also can feed their Manx jellied medicines to help hairballs pass harmlessly in the cat's waste.

Health Problems

Manx cats generally are very healthy. Manx can live for 15 to 20 years.

Manx cats born with tails can develop problems with their tails. The tail bones may grow together. A Manx also may develop

This longhaired Manx, or Cymric, may require daily brushing to prevent hairballs and mats.

arthritis in its tail. Both of these problems cause the tail to become stiff. To prevent these problems, breeders often cut off kittens' tails when they are a few days old. This practice is called docking. Tailless Manx also are more attractive to buyers.

Many articles and books discuss Manx Syndrome. They describe Manx Syndrome as several problems supposedly associated with the Manx gene for taillessness. Some people blame this gene for causing cats to develop spines that are too short. They also blame this gene for causing damaged nerves. This damage would result in weak back legs and a lack of bowel and bladder control.

Many Manx breeders and veterinarians say that there is no such thing as Manx Syndrome. They point out that these problems can occur in other breeds, not just Manx. The Manx gene for taillessness only affects the very end of the spine where the tail starts. It does not cause the spine to be too short.

Veterinarian Visits

Manx cats should be checked regularly by a veterinarian. Most veterinarians recommend that cats have yearly checkups. Older cats may need to visit the veterinarian more often. Older cats are more likely to develop health problems. Frequent checkups help the veterinarian find and treat these problems.

An owner who adopts a Manx cat or kitten should check its medical history. Manx that have not recently been to the veterinarian may need to see one. The veterinarian will check

Veterinarians recommend that Manx cats get yearly checkups to prevent or treat health problems.

the cat's heart, lungs, internal organs, eyes, ears, mouth, and coat.

Kittens often have their first vaccinations when they are ready to be adopted. The veterinarian will give the Manx any vaccinations it still needs. These shots of medicine help prevent diseases. These diseases include rabies, feline panleukopenia, and feline leukemia.

Manx cats can make loyal companions.

Rabies is a deadly disease that is spread by animal bites. Most states and provinces have laws that require owners to vaccinate their cats against rabies.

Feline panleukopenia also is called feline distemper. This virus causes fever, vomiting, and death.

Feline leukemia attacks a cat's immune system. The cat is unable to fight off infections and other illnesses. This disease is spread through a cat's bodily fluids. Owners who bring their cats to shows often vaccinate the animals against feline leukemia.

Cats should receive some vaccinations each year. Other vaccinations are given less often.

Veterinarians also can spay and neuter cats. These surgeries make it impossible for cats to breed. Owners who are not planning to breed their Manx should have them spayed or neutered. These surgeries prevent the birth of unwanted kittens. They also help prevent diseases of the reproductive organs. Spayed and neutered cats usually have calmer personalities than cats that do not have the surgeries.

Regular visits to the veterinarian are an important part of cat ownership. Owners and veterinarians should work together to help Manx cats live long, healthy lives. Owners and their Manx companions can have many years together.

RUMPY MANX

Round
head

Short
front legs

Quick Facts about Cats

A male cat is called a tom. A female cat is called a queen. A young cat is called a kitten. A family of kittens born at one time is called a litter.

Origin: Shorthaired cat breeds descended from a type of African wildcat called *Felis lybica*. Longhaired breeds may have descended from Asian wildcats. People domesticated or tamed these breeds as early as 1500 B.C.

Types: The Cat Fanciers' Association accepts 40 domestic cat breeds for competition. The smallest breeds weigh about 5 to 7 pounds (2.3 to 3.2 kilograms) when grown. The largest breeds can weigh more than 18 pounds (8.2 kilograms). Cat breeds may be either shorthaired or longhaired. Cats' coats can be a variety of colors. These colors include many shades of white, black, gray, brown, and red.

Reproduction: Most cats are sexually mature at 5 or 6 months. A sexually mature female cat goes into estrus several times each year. Estrus also is called "heat." During this time, she can mate with a male. Kittens are born about 65 days after breeding. An average litter includes four kittens.

Development: Kittens are born blind and deaf. Their eyes open about 10 days after birth. Their hearing develops at the same time. They can live on their own when they are 6 weeks old.

Life span: With good care, cats can live 15 or more years.

Sight: A cat's eyesight is adapted for hunting. Cats are good judges of distance. They see movement more easily than detail. Cats also have excellent night vision.

Hearing: Cats can hear sounds that are too high for humans to hear. A cat can turn its ears to focus on different sounds.

Smell: A cat has an excellent sense of smell. Cats use scents to establish their territories. Cats scratch or rub the sides of their faces against objects. These actions release a scent from glands between their toes or in their skin.

Taste: Cats cannot taste as many foods as people can. For example, cats are not very sensitive to sweet tastes.

Touch: Cats' whiskers are sensitive to touch. Cats use their whiskers to touch objects and sense changes in their surroundings.

Balance: Cats have an excellent sense of balance. They use their tails to help keep their balance. Cats can walk on narrow objects without falling. They usually can right themselves and land on their feet during falls from short distances.

Communication: Cats use many sounds to communicate with people and other animals. They may meow when hungry or hiss when afraid. Cats also purr. Scientists do not know exactly what causes cats to make this sound. Cats often purr when they are relaxed. But they also may purr when they are sick or in pain.

Words to Know

cartilage (KAR-tuh-lij)—a strong, rubbery tissue that connects bones in people and animals

Cymric (KIM-rick)—a longhaired Manx; some cat associations consider the Cymric to be a separate breed from the Manx.

euthanize (YOO-thuh-nize)—to put an animal to death by injecting it with a substance that stops its breathing or heartbeat

genetic mutation (juh-NET-ik myoo-TAY-shun)—a change in an animal's genetic makeup that causes it to develop in a different way

neuter (NOO-tur)—to remove a male animal's testicles so it cannot reproduce

spay (SPAY)—to remove a female animal's uterus and ovaries so it cannot reproduce

vaccination (vak-suh-NAY-shun)—a shot of medicine that protects a person or animal from disease

veterinarian (vet-ur-uh-NER-ee-uhn)—a doctor who is trained to treat the illnesses and injuries of animals

To Learn More

Alderton, David. *Cats.* Eyewitness Handbooks. New York: DK Publishing, 2000.

Commings, Karen. *Manx Cats: Everything about Purchase, Care, Nutrition, Grooming, and Behavior.* A Complete Pet Owner's Manual. Hauppauge, N.Y.: Barron's Educational Series, 1999.

Fogle, Bruce. *The New Encyclopedia of the Cat.* New York: DK Publishing, 2001.

Petras, Kathryn, and Ross Petras. *Cats: 47 Favorite Breeds, Appearance, History, Personality and Lore.* Fandex Family Field Guides. New York: Workman Publishing, 1997.

You can read articles about Manx cats in *Cat Fancy*.

Useful Addresses

American Cat Fanciers Association (ACFA)
P.O. Box 1949
Nixa, MO 65714-1949

Canadian Cat Association (CCA)
289 Rutherford Road South
Unit 18
Brampton, ON L6W 3R9
Canada

Cat Fanciers' Association (CFA)
P.O. Box 1005
Manasquan, NJ 08736-0805

The International Cat Association (TICA)
P.O. Box 2684
Harlingen, TX 78551

Internet Sites

American Veterinary Medical Association
http://www.avma.org/care4pets

Canadian Cat Association
http://www.cca-afc.com

Cat Fanciers' Association
http://www.cfainc.org

Cats Central
http://www.cats-central.com

The International Cat Association (TICA)
http://www.tica.org

The Mann Cat Sanctuary
http://www.manncat.com/index.html

Index

animal shelter, 21, 23–25, 26

breeders, 21–23, 26, 35, 36
breed standard, 17–18

cartilage, 7, 17
Cat Fanciers' Association, 9, 15, 18
cat show, 15, 17, 18, 21, 22
claw, 31–32
color, 18
Cymric, 9

disease, 31, 37–39

food, 29–30
fur, 9, 18, 33–34
    longhair, 9, 18, 33–34.
        See also Cymric
    shorthair, 9, 18, 33

genetic mutation, 12–13
grooming, 33–34

hairball, 34

Isle of Man, 11, 12, 15
litter box, 31

Manx Syndrome, 35–36
myth, 11–12

personality, 7, 9, 39

registration, 21, 26
rescue organization, 21, 25–26

scratching, 31

tail, 7–8, 11, 12, 13, 17, 18, 34–35, 36
    longy, 7–8
    riser, 7
    rumpy, 7
    stumpy, 7–8
teeth, 29, 33

vaccination, 37–39
veterinarian, 30, 33, 34, 36–37, 39

weight, 8